FIRST CAME THE SUMERIANS THEN THE AKKADIANS

Ancient History for Kids
Children's Ancient History

BABY PROFESSOR
EDUCATION KIDS

Speedy Publishing LLC

40 E. Main St. #1156

Newark, DE 19711

www.speedypublishing.com

Copyright 2017

Mesopotamia, the land between the Tigris and Euphrates rivers was controlled by the Sumerian Empire and then by the Akkadians. Who were they, and how were they different? Let's find out.

CONTROL OF MESOPOTAMIA

The richest area in the Middle East is Mesopotamia, the territory in what is now Iraq between the Tigris and Euphrates rivers. This is where farming developed so successfully that people could afford to build houses and live in them instead of following their herds from place to place.

Euphrates River

Ur

Many cultures and nations grew up in Mesopotamia, and often they struggled with each other over who would control the good land and good water supplies. The cultures that ended up on top, even for a while, influenced all the cultures and empires that came after them—and there have been a lot! Among the oldest cultures we know of are the Sumerians and the Akkadians.

THE SUMERIANS

The Sumerians emerged as a culture and civilization around 4000 BCE. Their original territory was very small, about fifty square miles, and held just a few cities.

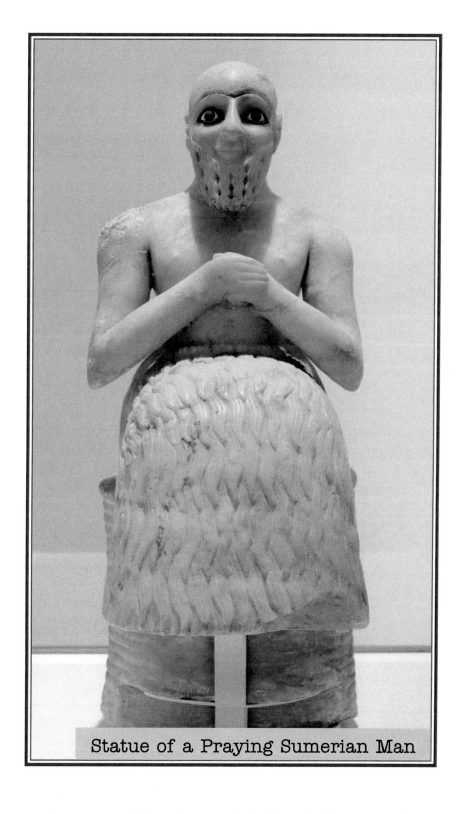

Statue of a Praying Sumerian Man

Sumerian Kingdom of Lagash

For the Sumerians, like the ancient Greeks, the city-state was the basic unit of government and economics. The kingdom was a weak collection of the city-states, and mainly operated to deal with an external threat to one or all of the cities. This meant the kingdom could defend itself, but was not in a good situation to expand.

The two key buildings in a Sumerian city were its temple and its palace. The temple was not just a place of worship. It was also where people brought their surplus grain and other goods, and came to find goods they needed. Workers creating woven cloth, or weapons or tools with metal edges, would bring them to the temple to find people who wanted to buy them.

The Sumerian word for "palace" means "big household". The palace was not only where the king or city ruler lived. Probably many members of the nobility lived there as well, and scribes and tax-gatherers would have their offices in the palace complex.

As Sumeria grew in population and wealth, the strength of its king grew. People believed that the kings were descended from people sent by the gods from heaven. The list of kings includes people like Gilgamesh, who may have actually existed, but who in the list is king for almost a thousand years. Learn more about Gilgamesh in the Baby Professor book The Sumerians' Writing System and Literature.

Gilgamesh Statue

Akkadian Cylinder Seal

THE AKKADIANS TAKE OVER

Around 3000 BCE the Akkadian people started moving into Mesopotamia from the west. They were able to gain control of the region.

Akkadian became the official language, not only of the Akkadian Empire, but of much of the Middle East. It was much easier to write than the earlier script the Sumerians had used. The Sumerian language continued, but it was confined to important documents and proclamations.

Akkadians

Ziggurat

It was sort of like how Latin was in western Europe after the fall of the Roman Empire: a language nobody spoke in everyday life, but that a lot of people in different regions understood well enough that they could use it to communicate with people who did not speak their local language.

Although the Akkadians were in power, we have no evidence of resentment or racial tension between them and the Sumerians. The Akkadians started calling themselves "the black-headed people", but nowhere is that term used like an insult.

Akkadians Ornately Depicted Hair

One difference was that, in northern Mesopotamia under the Akkadians, the palace and the king were the most important elements in society. In the southern part of the region, the temple was stronger, and the local ruler was seen as a servant of the chief local god

Around 2350 BCE the Akkadian ruler was Sargon. His real name was probably something else, because "sargon" in Akkadian means "this king is legitimate". He ruled for over fifty years, and greatly expanded the empire's boundaries.

Sargon of Akkad

Sargon

Sargon forced the Sumerian city-states into greater obedience, and gained territory for the kingdom in what is now Syria and eastern Turkey. Some historians say this expansion marks the beginning of the very first human empire!

The whole region under the Akkadians used the same system of weights and measures, and they called each month of the year by the same name. But the kings after Sargon had trouble keeping many parts of the empire, including Sumeria, in line.

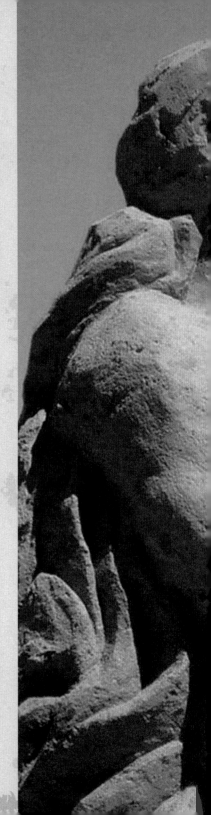

Sumerians

Victory Stele of Naram Sin

Sargon's grandson took the kingship to a whole new level: in writings about him, the scribes used a little symbol before his name. The symbol means "the next word is the name of a god." King Naram Sin was probably the first king to claim not only to be a servant of the gods, but to be one of them!

Under the Akkadians, artists and builders created striking work, although we only have fragments of large statues and many smaller pieces. One remarkable piece is a life-size statue in copper of a man sitting in a chair; another is a portrait in bronze that may be of Naram Sin. The Akkadians' final capital is buried under sand somewhere in the region. If we ever find it, we may find many more art treasures.

Victory Stele of Naram Sin

The Conquest of the Amorites

THE FALL OF THE AKKADIANS

The Akkadians spent a lot of time dealing with rebellions inside the empire. However, the blow that brought the Akkadians down was probably an invasion from the north. The Gutians, a people from what is now central Russia, invaded Mesopotamia not long after the death of Naram Sin and conquered the Akkadian Empire. At the same time the Amorites, from the west, captured some Akkadian territory.

Even though the Gutians were in control, from around 2100 BCE the city-states started to regain their old power. Sumer, and the Sumerian kingdom, were among them.

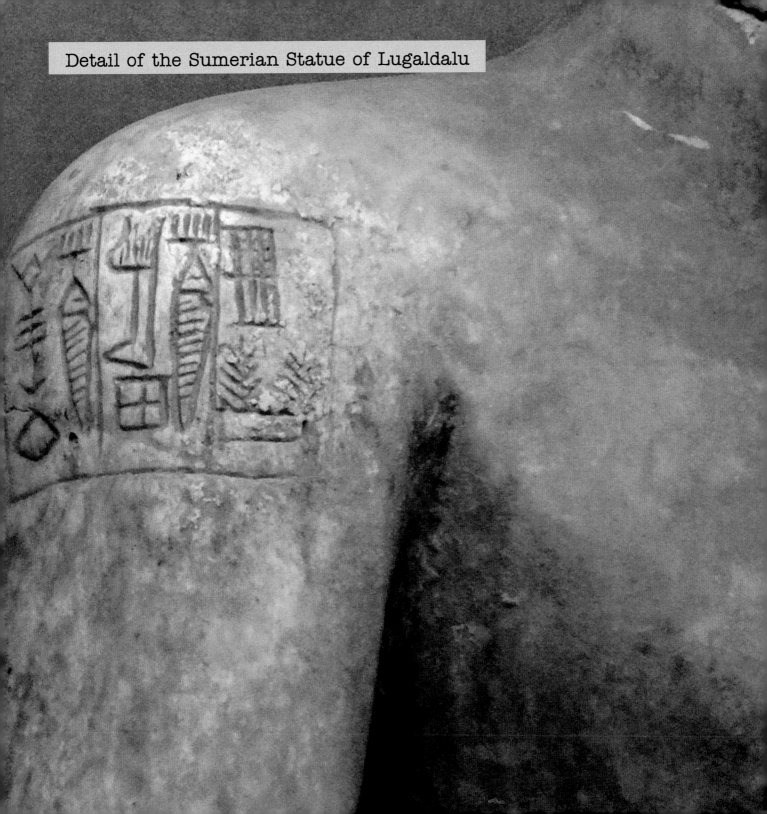
Detail of the Sumerian Statue of Lugaldalu

Inscribed Brick of King Ur-Nammu

A LAST SUMERIAN KINGDOM

Ur Nammu took power in the city of Ur as its king, and created a Sumerian dynasty that continued for over one hundred years. His memorial inscriptions claim that Ur Nammu drove the last of the Gutians out of the region.

Under Ur Nammu and his dynasty, Sumerian again became the official language of the region. His son, Shulgi, published the oldest code of laws that we know of, a code that influenced the famous Code of Hammurabi later in Babylon.

Hammurabi

Ur

This Sumerian kingdom made use of many features the Akkadians had developed, including how to administer the kingdom and giving their king status as a member of the gods. Shulgi was king for almost fifty years, and this gave him time to put in place many reforms to government, to the army, and even to how business was done in the kingdom.

Shulgi appointed local governors, reporting directly to him, who had the key job of preventing rebellion in their areas. The kingdom had a system of mounted messengers to carry news to the king and orders from him back to the regional leaders. You can read about a version of this in United States history in the Baby Professor book: Before FedEx there was the Pony Express.

Tablet of Shulgi

One of the most interesting things about this late Sumerian Empire is that tens of thousands of clay tablets have survived. The tablets show the careful record-keeping of a huge administration, taking note of cattle sales, delivery of wheat, and which temple should get which offerings in the current month.

Other tablets give fascinating details about how people planted and harvested their crops, how they dug canals for irrigation and for transport, and what the rules were for towing boats on the canals. There are a lot of details about the weaving centers where cloth was made. We know from the tablets that a herd that gave the wool might have as many as ten thousand sheep! The tablets also describe taking care of forests, making pots, and creating weapons, tools, and statues from metal.

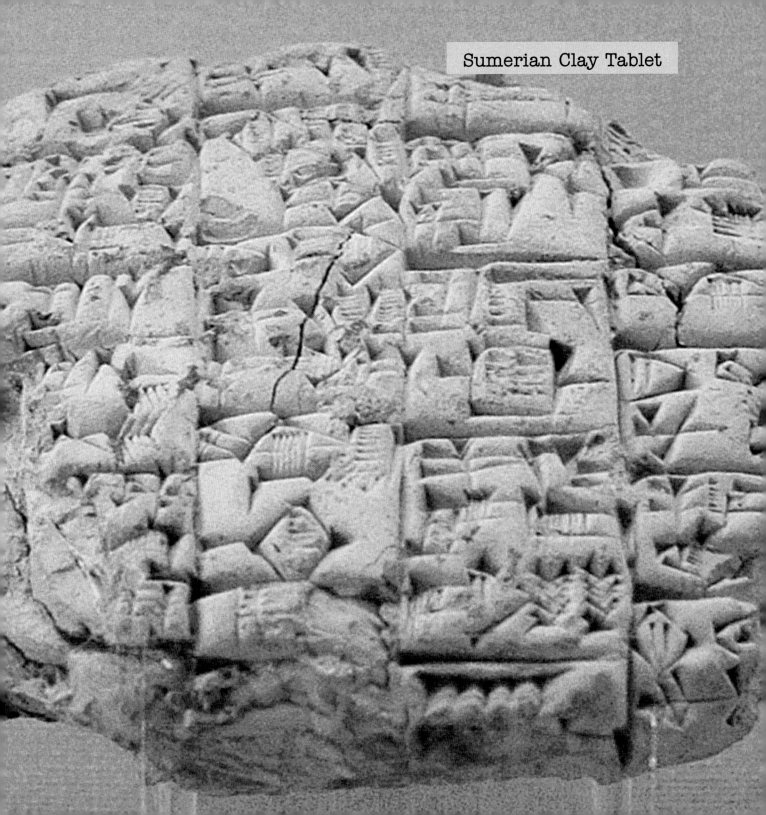
Sumerian Clay Tablet

Shulgi Tablet

We can even learn about Shulgi himself! According to writings about him, he could not only read and write Sumerian; he could speak four other languages. He was a famous athlete: one time he ran from the city of Ur to the holy city of Nippur and back again. That would be a greater distance than an Olympic marathon! He claimed to have swum across the Euphrates river.

Pressure from the Amorites to the west caused one of Shulgi's sons to build a defensive wall, like the Great Wall of China, to slow down the invaders (read about that larger and more successful structure in the Baby Professor book Who Built the Great Wall of China?).

Army of the Amorites

Elamite Rock

From the south of what is now Iran another people, the Elamites, began to press in. The kings began to lose control of their outer provinces, and then of the city-states closer to the center. When a famine struck the land, the kingdom did not have the resources to respond to it while keeping out the invading forces. By around 2000 BCE, the last Sumerian king was captured and its last empire had ended.

THE MANY MESOPOTAMIAN EMPIRES

The peoples of Mesopotamia and their empires are many. There's the Persian Empire and the Assyrian Empire. Each of these empires contributed to the rich history of Mesopotamia. The great King Hammurabi and his Code of Law brought about a major change in the country's history too.

Learn more about Mesopotamia and its many empires by reading other Baby Professor Books.

Visit

BABY PROFESSOR
EDUCATION KIDS

www.BabyProfessorBooks.com

to download Free Baby Professor eBooks
and view our catalog of new and exciting
Children's Books

Made in the USA
Monee, IL
06 October 2023